Love & Memory

Poems by Jamal Gabobe

Credits:
Front cover "Faces of Africa" © 1990 Sultan Mohamed
Interior illustrations © 1990 Sultan Mohamed
Author portrait back cover © 1996 Peter Makarkey
Cover design Scott C. Davis

"Love and Memory"
© Jamal Gabobe 1997
ISBN 1-885942-00-1-X

Reprinted in 2025 ISBN 978-1-61457-361-6

Bridge Between the Cultures (a series from Cune Press)	
Old enough to Know	Alice Rothchild
Kivu	Frederic Hunter
Empower a Refugee	Patricia Martin Holt
Biblical Time Out of Mind	Tom Gage, James A. Freeman
The Other Side of the Wall	Richard Hardigan
Apartheid Is a Crime	Mats Svensson
Curse of the Achille Lauro	Reem al-Nimer
Escape to Aswan	Amal Sedky Winter
Finding Melody Sullivan	Alice Rothchild
Mulsims, Arabs & Arab Americans	Nawar Shora

 Cune Press: www.cunepress.com

Contents

Love

I	9
II	11
III	13
IV	15
V	17
VI	19
VII	21
VIII	23
IX	25
X	27
XI	29
Dead End	31

Memory

About the man Somalis call Big Mouth	39
A question for my father	41
Of fish and fishermen	43
The year of death	45
Big Mouth's fourteenth anniversary	47
The dictator's modus operandi	49
Commentary	53

© 1996 Sultan Mohamed

Love

I

And we think there is always a way
to where we are not.
If this, if that, we say
if only we could touch.
Forgetting that touching is not only
with the hands.

II

And every time I think of
what I have missed
I sigh.
Every time I cannot remember something
I should
I die.
Yes, I have checked out the American girls in their prime.
They checked me too,
felt me as an idle dream, as a question
without an answer.
And why should I blame them?
I, too, have often felt that way about myself.
This homeless, hopeless self.
This *I* with nothing to back it up.

III

In our metallic bed, we wrestle.
Part of the sheets around us, part underneath us
part lost, like us.
As we try to connect our desires
the gap between us widens.
We do it any way
like two robots doing what they must.
When it's over, you light a cigarette.
I turn on the TV.
Neither of us can bear to look at the other.

IV

After so many false starts, defeats,
our patience dries out.
We no longer care
about what note we have missed
or if our alliance serves any purpose.
Escaping time and its troubles,
we slide into an ancient madness.
We have inherited a kingdom of salt,
with all its wicked glory.
Erosion at the periphery, numbness in the center-
it's what we get for going around in circles.

V

Wild, impure rain, pours.
A weary sea makes no attempt to meet it
even half way.
The rain keeps coming.
Unable to welcome it
or drive it away
the sea dissolves it.
Makes it part of itself.
Rain and sea become one.

A leaf on the grass becomes a new diversion
for my wanton eyes.
Some of its veins are still there,
some are gone, and some are slowly thinning out.
The outcome is a foregone conclusion
but even then, there's a difference
in how one faces the inevitable.

VI

To walk and not feel
the ground.
To think and not see
the thoughts.
My life, broken into so many pieces
there's no point in counting.
But despite my condition, I had to come to some decision.
After saying no so many times
I finally say what the heck.
What can I do with burning lips, but bite them.

VII

Jawboned by desire
I make an attempt to fill my cup
of her temporary kindness.
More want is my reward.
I should have known better-
that in the economics of desire
supply never equals demand.

—Seattle, 1982-1986

VIII

Night is here
and the day is behind me.
Time to forget you say.
I agree.
I want to forget
today's troubles
and everything else.
But they won't forget me.
Today's noose is tightening
around my neck.
And I must live with these and
a thousand other daily hurts,
the hurt of being studied, catalogued,
and filed away.
The hurt of small comforts
costing so much.
And the bitter knowledge that by talking about
my troubles
I bring them back to life, become an accomplice.
Believe me, there's no joy in being clawed like this,
and I would rather forget.
But every time I try, I find myself
reliving the baseness of the periphery and center.

IX

I know these words are nothing
compared to the real thing;
to you, and me, and the southern nights
but they are all I have.
The only thing left.
Mere words and memory.
I remember the pattern.
It's burned into me.
Hours of idleness.
It's perilous to talk of these things
but after the wreck, what have I got to lose?
With deprivation a constant companion,
my will punctured,
so flat, so useless.
Now, do you see where these words are coming from?
Why though they are a cheap substitute
I keep using them?
Why everything begins and ends with you.

X

Yesterday, I asked myself that same old question:
why do I keep going back to the beginning, to her?
As usual I had no answer.
Earlier today I asked myself this same question
there was no answer either.
I am asking this question now
still no answer.
It is tempting to take a guess or two
but I won't.
Too much is at stake.
All I know is that I am going back.

XI

And we always want to be
where we are not.
We want to be back
to the beginning.
To feel one more time
the delirium of discovery.
We find out how foolish we are
making such impossible demands.
And we fall back on the only thing left:
memory.

—Seattle, 1987-1990

Dead End

In a matter of days, it will be my thirteenth year here
and more than ever I am lifeless.
Like the rest of you, I once had a home, a country,
but no more.

I remember late one night the door being kicked,
an officer yelling, "*Meeye Xunki. Halkaad ku qarinaysa?*"
And my terrified mother whimpering, "*Mooyi. Wali mu iman.*"
He pushed her aside, ordered his jackbooted thugs to look
everywhere, and when they could not find me, he promised next
time I wouldn't be so lucky,
and stormed out of the house.
Home was no longer home.

In many ways though I am like everyone else.
I hold a job, go out on weekends, love baseball
and that is not even the half of it.
Linda bless her heart used to say:
"It must be hard speaking a different language:'
She was right.
Still, many times I wanted to tell her
there was more to language than mere speech;
that no tongue tastes like another.
But I didn't.
How could I, with her being so kind to me?

In a way I am even privileged,
for how many people get shitcanned
by more than one country?

I tell you, there are so many things I want to forget.
Like, for instance, the first cousin who was bayoneted to death
by soldiers, when he refused to let them take his watch.
Not long after that, I mailed his picture to an arms manufacturer
here in this great city
with a note: Human Sacrifice.

It is not that I like to dwell on things like this.
No, I was not always like this.
I keep telling myself, it's time to put this thing behind you.
Time to move on.
But as soon as I say this, I am back to square one.
One more thing about Linda,
and this is not going to win me any points,
but I did promise to tell the truth:
I made it with her sister.
She kept insisting on teaching me skiing;
Linda did not object.
She even added, "you may like if"
Well, I did.
First we slid down the snow,
then nearby, it was her and I naked,
with the forest reeking of our lust.

Of course that's no way to reward kindness.
But how could I have known
there was more to the offer than skiing?
To betray or be betrayed, why does it always come to this?
To say in one tongue what belongs to another,
isn't that also a kind of betrayal?

As I search for the right words, the appropriate phrase,
pick a fight with one verb, make peace with another,
try to master the secrets of this stubborn language,
resist being overwhelmed by its sheer weight,
and above all, tell my story.
Or is this too much to ask for?

When I told a friend of mine that I am writing my story, he answered:
"There's already enough sadness in the world:'
Was he right?
Am I only bringing more sadness into the world?

And yet, I do know that since I have lost one war,
it is my destiny to fight another-of verbs, nouns,
syntax, grammar.
How much I hated grammar,
and here I'm again face to face with it:
the comma versus the period, the question mark and its allies,
a war against an army of metaphors
tearing me into a thousand pieces, leaving me without a center.

But oddly enough, it was also then that I discovered certain things about myself,
how widespread is the rot.
My first instinct was to cover it up, hide it.
It didn't work.
So, I went on the offensive, started digging up my own dirt, rubbing myself with it,
accepting it as an integral part of me.
It almost worked.
But as I'm absorbed with myself, other thoughts intrude,
and I say to myself, your plight is nowhere as bad
as the dear aunt, who first lost her only son to a land mine,
then lost her mind.
She still engages in these long conversations with him to this day,
as if he were still around, as if nothing happened.
Her mind was stretched beyond its limit.
Unable to find comfort in the present, she ransacks the past.
Sometimes, I ask myself, if I have also reached that point?

I tell myself, once, there were so many natives on this very land.
Now calling them a minority is considered doing them a favor.
History is such a bitch.

It's past midnight in this pub, and the pain I came here
to get rid of is still with me.
The fire, in this artificial fireplace, is still raging,
breaks into so many colors,
with phosphoric blue at its center.
The bartender abruptly turns off the jukebox,
announcing, "Is Bob here?"
The guy behind me protests, "I paid for it:'
Someone else declares, "Wallace Stevens was dishonest.
He had a job he could always go back to:'
I came here to escape, instead
everyday I face another death.

—Seattle, March 25, 1990

An excerpt from this poem appeared in the *University of Washington Daily*, October 25, 1990.

Memory

About the man Somalis call Big Mouth

He is a man who thinks he is not like other men.
Sometimes, he thinks he is a fish.
As he told his eldest son:
"Life is no more unpredictable, no more demanding than the sea.
We all know what eventually happens to men,
but have you ever heard of a fish that drowned?"

Sometimes he thinks he is a chameleon.
As he told that same son:
"Be the first to figure the wind's direction;
then set your sails to it.
you know what they say about survival, who survives
and who doesn't."

Other times he is a vulture.
As he told his son:
"There's no greater asset than a sharp nose,
spares you from doing any real work.
Don't mind how rotten is a corpse,
as they say: one man's meat is another's poison:'

But most of the time, he would rather not think at all.
As he told that same son:
'avoid thinking as much as you can.
Questions without answers
mirages and mirrors

breeding doubt, confusion,
a weakling's fare.
The secret of power is in the strength of your hands:'

—Portland, 1984.

Big Mouth is the nickname of the Somali ex-dictator, Mohammed Siyad Barre, who ruled Somalia from October 21, 1969 until January, 1991. His corrupt, divisive, and brutal reign was largely responsible for the killing of thousands of civilians in the north, the famine in the south, and the disintegration of the country.

A question for my father

O strange one whose face is an ancient text.
0 sad one who stoically endures the vagaries of time.
0 happy one who delights in the deadly silence
at the core of all things.
Why do I feel so wounded, so weak?

—Vancouver, B.C., 1989.

Note: My father, may God have mercy on his soul, was a businessman and a devoted family man who believed in discipline, duty, and sacrifice. For many years, as I was trying to find my voice as a poet, I thought I had failed to measure up to his standards. This caused me a great deal of anguish. He was also a mystic, a part of him which has fascinated me since my childhood. I wrote this poem before he passed away in April 2, 1995, in Hargeisa, Somaliland.

Of fish and fishermen

Amazing is the patience of these fishermen.
They sit for hours.
Unfazed by the turbulent mood of the sea,
focused on that moment of contact
between two kinds of hunger.
Amazing is this fanatic dedication
to what the future may or may not bring.

—Seattle, 1980.

The year of death

Over there, in my ancestral home
an orgy of bones and blood is unleashed.
Some are jailed.
Some disappear.
Others are shot.
A common grave as big as the sun has been dug.
And the world is silent.
Over there, in the African Horn,
sick hearts seek relief in the language of bullets.
Bodies are crushed.
And for the zillionth time, a crude fact is confirmed: flesh and bones are no match for bullets.

That's the news.
A not so new news.
And the world is silent.
So I get sick.

The bottle and pills make me only sicker.
I write some letters.
Make a few calls.
Tell what happened.
What the cannibals in fatigues did.
Tell about men, women, and children who were bombed in their homes,
and then bombed again as they fled.
'Til I am sicker than sick,
and can't tell one death from another.

'Til I, myself, become a vehicle of death.
It has truly been a year of negation.
The year of death.
And the world is silent.

Note: I wrote this poem in reaction to President Barre's massacre of civilians in the northwestern part of Somalia, in May 27-3 l, 1988. As a result of Barre's relentless brutality, this part of the country has seceded from the rest of Somalia, and is now known as The Somaliland Republic.

Big Mouth's fourteenth anniversary

Another year has passed and you're still in our lives.
Still wearing a crown carved of our sorrow.
You strut on the stage, with signs of your success all around you.
It must be reassuring,
having so much money, power, prestige;
and what's most important to you: giving orders, not taking them.
You look so happy, satisfied.

Clearly, you have surpassed yourself.
But do you remember how it began?
You probably forgot, or more likely don't want to remember. (I can see you shouting some things should not be remembered.)
So, let me remind you.
You won for two reasons: our frustration with your predecessors, and your sweet promises.
You knew we were impatient, unhappy, naive.
And that's when you struck.
You told us, after the fact, that you did it for us.
And you promised, yes you promised, that you will be different,
that you'll take care of us,
and we believed you.
We never even bothered to look closely at you, or your record; that's how desperate we were;
how much we were looking for someone, anyone, to believe, to save us from ourselves.
And you were so good with words.
You told us just what we wanted to hear.
You made us feel so good about ourselves.

In our dizziness we even ignored your past,
how you lap-dogged your Italian masters;
kowtowed to their fat women.
Though you were too old and used-up to be a hero,
we were willing to give you a new start.
In return we wanted fairness, common sense,
but you had neither.
Instead, you had something else: the element of surprise.

Every time we thought we had seen it all, you'd come up with a new one.
If anything was constant about you, it was this.
You spent most of your time trying to keep us off-balance. Well, congratulations, you've succeeded.

The dictator's modus operandi

First came the Russians.
"What can we do for you comrade?" they asked.
"Guns. Please give me guns, tanks, planes;' you answered. Guns they gave you, plus some.
You were so happy.
Guns are fun, you found out.
"I've finally arrived, and I dare any bastard to say otherwise;' you yelled.
"The evidence is there for everyone to see,
only the envious and the wicked would deny it;' you declared, pounding the table with your fist.
But you knew how to deal with them.
You had the whip, the blade, and the bullet
to take care of any mischief.
Since they wouldn't see the truth, it was only fair to make them taste it.
"Even the white infidels say: give to Caesar what's Caesar's;' you shouted.

Landcruisers, villas, diplomatic passports, and yes cash for loyal members of the tribe.
The rest were locked out.
To you, it only made sense, that it should be so.
There were only two types of people in your book: those who obeyed, and those who didn't.
Through the iron bars we could still see your new order,
the work in progress, a new genre reconciling east and west. Damn Kipling, what did he know.

Yes, they did meet, but the result was not a tragedy but farce:
The American Ambassador calling you again and again, begging to see you about a planned joint-military exercise to cement the fraternal ties, and you screaming at your secretary: "tell the bastard I'm not here:'

You changed your ministers, your watchdogs, your mistresses, so often;
everyone is dispensable, everything is negotiable, except who sits on the throne.
You made that so clear.
And then came your master stroke which would have made Caligula envious: You made your mulish brother a minister.
At first, we thought it was a joke;
but we quickly discovered it wasn't.
You fooled us again.

I remember one time dozing-off while you gave a speech,
and when I woke, you were still at it.
I wanted to leave the stadium, but I knew better.
Words were flying out of your mouth, stretching, contracting, hanging in the air;
your jesters in khaki keeping their criminal eyes on everyone, elated to take part in your freak show.
You kept on.
More words, slogans, cliches,
trying to keep up with your own slippery mouth;
I looked again at the clock, but it was obvious you wouldn't stop; as if doing so would be the end of the world, defeat.
And you abhorred nothing more than defeat.
To you, it was worse than death.
Sir, you're a genius.
You've achieved the impossible: words have lost their meaning.

"Power is the greatest aphrodisiac;' said one famous statesman. "There's power and there's power;' you replied.
You knew which is which.

You've had your day in the sun, but here I am
living day-to-day, afraid of what might be next,
my heart frostbitten by grief.
And there is no end in sight.
Wishes, promises, they have all come to naught.

You feed your fires with our flesh, get high on its stench,
then you rail, "What's the matter with these bastards?"
I saw your rage, but could not understand it.
This was, of course, before I knew
one could get used to anything.
Before I knew, history starts and ends with blood,
and I must crawl my way out of it.

But then you get to a point where it does not matter
whether blood is gushing from history's ears or ass.
History is history, that should be enough;
and its sword should not be constantly at our throat.

But first, I had to learn how to live on the surface of things. How to
make home and hearth out of the flimsiest elements.
This is what I've come to.

I spend so much time figuring ways to escape
my past, present, myself.
Once, there was a promise, but now I know there is no promised-land.
Still, I keep at it-a cornered instinct egging me on:
run, man, run,
another part of me begging for relief.
How could there be so much chaos in one life?

Commentary

I wrote these poems during the 1980s. I was living in the United States where I felt isolated, homesick, and disturbed by constant reports of brutality by the military regime in Somalia. I was at a low point. You could say I was going through an intellectual, spiritual, and emotional crisis.

During this period I was also preoccupied with the question of my own identity. I was born in one place, raised in another, and now found myself living in the big U. S. of A. In other words, I was trying to reconcile my Somaliness with my other identities and with my American experience.

It was a most difficult task, full of failure and disappointment. I was torn by contradictory thoughts and feelings. I came dangerously close to the edge. But somehow I went on. A sad story, but I am still here, and one good thing came of it: these poems.

Jamal Gabobe was born in Somaliland in 1957, raised in Aden (Yemen), and now lives in Seattle where he studies comparative literature at the University of Washington. He is one of the founders of The Internationals, a Seattle underground poetry project. He has written a novel, a play, and is currently working on a nonfiction book about Somalis. His essay "Termites and Clans" is featured in the collection An Ear to the Ground: Presenting Writers from 2 Coasts (Cune).

About Cune Press

Cune Press was founded in 1994 to publish thoughtful writing of public importance. Our name is derived from "cuneiform." (In Latin *cuni* means "wedge.")

In the ancient Near East the development of cuneiform script—simpler and more adaptable than hieroglyphics—enabled a large class of merchants and landowners to become literate. Clay tablets inscribed with wedge-shaped stylus marks made possible a broad intermeshing of individual efforts in trade and commerce.

Cuneiform enabled scholarship to exist and art to flower, and created what historians define as the world's first civilization. When the Phoenicians developed their sound-based alphabet, they expressed it in cuneiform.

The idea of Cune Press is the democratization of learning, the faith that rarefied ideas, pulled from dusty pedestals and displayed in the streets, can transform the lives of ordinary people. And it is the conviction that ordinary people, trusted with the most precious gifts of civilization, will give our culture elasticity and depth—a necessity if we are to survive in a time of rapid change.

Books from Cune Press

Aswat: Voices from a Small Planet (a series from Cune Press)

Looking Both Ways	Pauline Kaldas
Stage Warriors	Sarah Imes Borden
Stories My Father Told Me	Helen Zughaib & Elia Zughaib
Girl Fighters	Carolyn Han
Escape to Aswan	Amal Sedky Winter
Sharazad's Gift	Gretchen McCullough
Jinwar	Alex Poppe

Syria Crossroads (a series from Cune Press)

Leaving Syria	Bill Dienst & Madi Williamson
Visit the Old City of Aleppo	Khaldoun Fansa
Steel & Silk	Sami Moubayed
Syria - A Decade of Lost Chances	Carsten Wieland
The Road from Damascus	Scott C. Davis
A Pen of Damascus Steel	Ali Ferzat
White Carnations	Musa Rahum Abbas
Dusk Visitor	Musa Al-Haloul

Bridge Between the Cultures (a series from Cune Press)

Empower a Refugee	Patricia Martin Holt
Biblical Time Out of Mind	Tom Gage, James A. Freeman
Afghanistan and Byond	Linda Sartor
The Other Side of the Wall	Richard Hardigan
Apartheid Is a Crime	Mats Svensson
Curse of the Achille Lauro	Reem al-Nimer
Finding Melody Sullivan	Alice Rothchild
Confessions of a Knight Errant	Gretchen McCullough
Muslims, Arabs & Arab Americans	Nawar Shora
Old Enough to Know	Alice Rothchild

Cune Press: www.cunepress.com

www.ingramcontent.com/pod-product-compliance
Lightning Source LLC
Chambersburg PA
CBHW070036040426
42333CB00040B/1693